AF397405

To myselves

Being a total

Dick

Dick Stunbolt

Table of contents:

You'll figure it out.

February 15th 2022

What the fuck am I doing here? It looks familiar. Did I have a good time? Apparently not. Seems the blood comes from my head. Hurts. Hell? Why not? Could be. But the darker and colder version. Reminds me of when I was arrested in Tijuana. Man! That was a really bad involuntary withdrawal. Cold damp stone walls closing in. Rats and bugs. Porridge. Agony. Little fucking birds chirping outside at the break of dawn. Mocking and laughing at me. Smug fuckers. I have to focus on positive thinking; I'm alive and it's quiet inside. They're sleeping.

"Shhh…don't move…!"

As this is a somewhat unfamiliar environment and I'm nearly naked, I've come to the conclusion that I left the institution. Come to think of it, the last recollection of it is the park. The nurse. The radio. And then; epiphany. Waking up to the sweetest rock n' roll, numbing all other outside impressions. I'm the Superstar and everything is about me. The crowd is going wild. I'm going wild. Scream for me! And they do. And it doesn't stop. It can't ever stop.

/Dick

1st Movement – My Head Exploded

Yes, I definitely walked out out that place. Got some smokes, the short, damp second hand kind with lipstick marks. Sweet. Felt my thoughts gathering again after living apart for too long. Like old friends reunited after a painful and forced time apart. I totally forgot all about living life. Suck the marrow out of it and all that shit. And music. This invisible force that may be the only thing coming to my battered and shattered soul's rescue. Suddenly realizing; I have endless ideas for new songs. I can just pick the cherries out of any reasonably recollected event of this life. I'm gonna tell the world my story and it will sound just as amazing as in my mind. I'm gonna do crazy shit, I guarantee!

Just need to get my hands on a guitar…

/Dick

February 17th 2022, Morning

Found a Les Paul in a dumpster! That's the sort of advantage you get, hanging out by a landfill. Also gave me the opportunity to suit up like a seventies vacuum cleaner door to door salesman. Made a fabulous one hand lick and was instantly filled with the urge to get a band together. Went to a pub. Immediately noticed people were just waiting for me to show. All in awe. And this is where my luck changed. As an impulse I sat down and bet the only coin in my possession. Formerly in the possession of the last unknown owner of the suit, more exactly. Went pretty well.

Soon enough I found myself throwing a shitload of cash in the air and was even interviewed by a local news crew covering the story on live tv. Drinks were on me. And that means liquor all over me. It's weird you know; the amount of cash in one's possession, corresponds like exactly to the level of attention and fame one experiences.

I can't lose, holy shit, I'm loaded! Is this really happening? Hard to tell since I've been told I have an overactive brain. Feels like my head exploded, which is a sensation I get a lot. Now, where is that guitar? Never mind, I can get ten more, easy. And a drum kit. Two drum kits. A whole drum factory, a guitar brand and a French vineyard. Maybe I can have a complete entourage of people following me around, taking care of the press, making hotel bookings and paying off the police. The latter is of course key if I want to be able to travel the world on the proper amount of drugs. And I want that. Or else I need to seriously dig into solving my mental issues, which I don't really feel like, nor have the time for.

Anyway, as soon as I'm drunk enough I'll split and get into the adventures I deserve! And you too, for that matter.

"You're with me?"
"We choose not to answer at this point."

/Dick

February 17th 2022, Afternoon

I now feel that I've come to a place in my life where I no longer feel the burden of owning properties or any other funds what so ever.

That means I'm broke. I was quite wealthy for a couple of hours. Now I'm not. And the guitar is gone. My luck changed back, I think. I know there isn't such a thing as luck. Things just happen. Sometimes you can affect events. For example fuck up royally. I do that often, but on the upside I do not get bored and that is of great importance to me. Feeling like shit, sure, but it's not boring. Not even in my darkest hour. I guess that's just the way I am. My mind is constantly stirring up the most fabulous forgotten impulses form the repressed depths, melting them together into pure gold. I'm the gold-cooking chef and everything I touch is like blessed by my presence. You might say I think too highly of myself, but what are you gonna do about it? Envious bastards. You can go fuck yourself! And while you do that I will for sure make rock n' roll history. Win- win.

/Dick

February 17th 2022, Hiding out

If you care a lot about consistency and chronology in a story, you might not come to consider yourself the target audience here, but bare with me. Infinitive, past simple and past participle are in a constant conflict in my head. I'll try to sort things out best I can, but you have to realize the damage done by the disgustingly large amounts of various central stimulant substances that have passed though my system the past, you know, life. Some health issues regarding my sanity and in particular the absence of impulse control, have not helped either. Life has not been a walk in the park. Gonna tell you all about it if you just hang in there.

So, as you might know, money comes and then you might lose it in a haze of liquor and gambling. I did that. In a top notch mobile casino I found myself going all in. Paper, rock & scissors is a fine game, but here I crashed hard. Not allowing myself to get too disappointed I instantly traded a bottle of whisky for a shotgun and demanded everyone to follow my lead.

"Let's go trick or treat", I shouted and was thrown out. Like I said, I went on and…it's a bit unclear, but it was like a movie and I could see myself from the outside. Entering a store in slow motion. I'm loaded. A hobo zombie with a shotgun looking for the opportunity to get his hands on some free vinyl classics. Feelin' like a nuclear battle ship. I think I was singing along with the soundtrack as I took an aim, graciously fell over and blasted a hole through the ceiling.

"Holy shit, it's loaded!"

I'm running. It's a manhunt, and I'm the man. Helicopter? I must be making the news again. A live covered relevant news story about a handsome, bare breasted dangerous but irresistibly likable hunk and his unequal fight against the injustices he wrongly faces. The average housewife's wet dream. Daytime television at its peak. They had no chance what so ever. I know these hoods better than anyone. Luring them into the old factory yard and then; gone. The hero vanishes into thin air. I could hear an awesome guitar solo being executed, just flawless. This is the starting point! I'm gonna record a song about this! Gonna use a Gibson for the solo part. Even if I myself mostly use Fender Stratocaster, I think this song has to have a more Les Paul type of sound to it. Maybe I'll use both. Left speaker – Les Paul. Right speaker – Stratocaster. Yes! That's it! Page and Hendrix on the same track. Jimmy & Jimi. And me! Have to get to work. Where's my gear? Not here anyway. I think I'm back where I started, or? Sure is cold and damp and my clothes are missing. They often inexplicably vanish from my body. What's up with that?

I'm listening to *Bitches Brew*. Or, I mean, inside I am. Don't have the record here, but I've memorized it. I can play it back in my head exactly as it is. For sure one of the top ten albums of all time, no doubt. What are the other nine…? Tricky. Sure to be included, in no particular order, are of course; *In Rock*, *Necropolis Transparent*, *Harvest*, *Are You Experienced*, *Moving Pictures*, *Necroticism – Descanting the Insalubrious*, *Held High*, *Human*, *Lulu…* The last one is a joke. Just to make you pay attention. Actually, it's surprisingly crappy, that one. One of rock history's worst moments. An utter shit show beyond belief. If it wasn't for that one, just maybe *Transformer* would have made the list. Now it's tainted forever. How many is that? And why just limit the list to ten? Can't I make the list as long as I want? Yes? No? I'll have to come back to this. There is one album in particular that for sure is going to make the list complete. An album which hasn't been made yet. That's my album. It will be self titled, obviously.
"A little louder…that's it! Thanks, Miles"
Pure perfection. It reminds me of myself.

/Dick

March 1st 2022, Still hiding

I recall a music video shoot I did with my old band back in -06. Me doing all lead vocals and occasionally some guitar. The band was founded in -98 by me and was called Stunningham's Great. I know we played a lot of shows which I do not remember. I fell off the wagon completely. I was only in it for the drugs at that point. Despite the name, it wasn't a great band, but the audience seemed to like it for some reason. Idiots. The band's sound was somewhere in the range between adult mainstream soft rock and *Hits for kids*. In particular a single called *Times we had* that I wrote, was popular at the time of its release. The song's lyrical content is a tragedy which involves a delusional depressed character who longs for his loved one's unconditional affection. The feeling is however not mutual. He is upset and his inner demons aid him in trying to convince her of the benefits of getting back together during an autumn walk in the forrest. Eventually this leads to a murder-suicide type of tragic ending. Easy listening made uncomfortable. I think I still have the master tape somewhere. Must have been originally released in -99, I think. So, for that video shoot some years later, the record label had forced us to suit up and made us bring all our gear to a film studio, in Osaka I believe. I can't recall for what song it was, though. Or what label it was, for that matter.

"It's important that the audience can see the amps and drums and everything, just like on stage", they said.

"We don't want to carry all that stuff", we said.

"Read the contract", they said.

"Well, is it really necessary?", we said.

"You will abide or hear from our lawyers. You will be in debt for the remaining days of your shitty lives", they said.

"See you on Monday then", we said.

Apparently some trashed hotel rooms and stolen gear from venues had caught up with us.

The atmosphere at the set was quite infected, as you might imagine. I got the feeling everyone was blaming me. They were probably not completely wrong in doing so. In the video, shot on 8mm film you can clearly notice the total absence of amps. The drums are shown, but that's just because Highman is sitting there waving his little sticks. The studio turned out to be too small for a four piece band and the edit is just showing separate shots for each member from the same angle. What were the other's names…? The dude with the studio and some other guy…? Can't find it. Nothing there. A few hours of filming, about halfway through, the sipping on beer started to evolve to heavy drinking and it was about lunchtime when I overdosed on smack. I was clinically dead for over three minutes. When I was discharged from the hospital three weeks later I had nothing. No band. No home. No friends. Purposeless. No plans for the future what so ever. I saw the music video just once. Without sound through the smudgy glass of a storefront. After that I never heard of Stunningham's Great again. I wonder if there's any fans still out there?

I haven't got a lot of memories from the time that followed. I know I got sick and I know I got weird. I started to have conversations with myself. Began to tell myself things. Sometimes I knew it wasn't real. But most of the time, and I was told this later, I followed the poor advice of characters my mind had created. At times I was like *in command*, just carrying out stupid tasks like burglary, theft and constantly insulting random people in the street. I lived my life inside my own mind. Never alone. I was forced to carry out orders from others, but when the shit hit the fan, I was always the only one taking the fall. They are some annoying fuckers, you know.

"But we love you…"

/Dick

This is Hell?

Love?

/Mother

March 3rd 2022

I love to skate. And drugs. Small wheels keep on rollin'. Rollin' down the street to the arcade which rolls back along the street to my home or what are you doing no no no how am I ever going to make it to the top of the pops with these pants keep me posted grandpa sitting in his chair watching the pigeons draft the best players to the little league holy mother I'm cold girls girls boys got me a fine specimen at the market best Fender Stratocaster I've ever played rollin' rollin' fallin' in love look out Dick it's me hey man what's up let's get the band together yeah what an excellent idea lets make a forced entry and occupy the theatre I'll bring the others and the backline remember to go with the flow take care see you Monday what's today it's springtime birds flowers blankets in the park bottles family day with the company telemarketing heaven just for me you and all those people over there rollin' rollin' callin' your sister and selling some crappy pearl necklace I stole a lot of those and sold them for illegal substances I hold dearly hey man it's tomorrow we're playing a show note to self bring costumes to the costume party and that gorilla friend of yours is she right in the head you think still goin' strong I promise to be there I'm here feels like my head exploded Dick.

April 12th 2022, Restroom

First I thought It was my funeral. But I was just sound asleep on the smudgy tiles where leaks have been taken by thousands of men for decades.

"Good morning, Dick", I heard myself say as I let myself go.

I was thinking about farm life and how bad that would fit me. Hard work, worrying about the fucking weather, smelling like shit every day, sick animals and being nice to idiot customers at the farmer's market on the weekends. Fun to drive the big machines though. I can apparently do that anyway. Just got myself a big ass tractor yesterday. Somehow found myself in the mud outside the city and there it was. Drove into the sunset and parked it outside a bar.

I think my notes have been mixed up and the dates are confusing. Might just be correct though. Since I can't really tell if the order of events add up, I'll just leave it as it is. What has been and what is taking place right now is not of any importance anyway. If you read this maybe you eventually get an aha-moment and it turns out to be one of those clever stories with fucked up timelines people love, giving them a moment to shine like Sherlock. I-knew-it-all-along type of stories that bring meaning to the average culture consuming enthusiast. So, now I planted that thought, spoiling the story for you. Good. I figure these notes will serve as background to the overlying goal of creating a musical adventure, featuring Richard Stunningham Bolthausen a.k.a. Dick Stunbolt, as the star and author of the only experience you'll ever need.

How does it start?

Right.

<u>Status check:</u>

Poorly dressed – check.

Probably self-inflicted head injury – check.

Financial ruin – check.

Ideas for timeless rock n' roll masterpiece – check.

Location – lost.

Let's begin!

/Dick

2nd Coming - Super Duper Megastar

Some time back, let's say before I lived rent free in my own head and before I was in custody of the state, given cups of pills to every meal, I had a life partner. Her name was A…started with an A…fuck it! I don't know. The only name that comes up is Antichrist. Let's call her that. Anyway. I had a life partner called Antichrist who I met at a meeting we both unwillingly attended. Same sentence, same judge. Since I am more of a Christ-like-Jesus-type of person than Antichrist, and as you know opposites attract, there was instantly a mutual understanding of wanting each other. It was clear that in this case it wasn't just the opposites, but definitely the similarities that attracted. We started to hit it off in the bathroom of such a meeting. I did more drugs in those meetings than at any party I ever attended. I soon moved into her apartment. All my stuff was there for years after I left her. We had a lot of fun, but mostly not. Don't remember how the relationship ended, but I recall a lot of disagreements and I recon I just didn't come home one day. She used to say "If you don't come back tomorrow, you don't have to ever set foot here again!" I bet she was worried sick and probably thought I was deceased. Sorry Antichrist. So much for background story! So, I'm half naked, cold and most definitively a wanted man. Where to go, if not to pay a long overdue visit to Antichrist. I was running up her street trying to revoke the memory of where I hid the emergency key all that time ago. I started to dig behind the trash can on the corner and suddenly it was there in my hand. By now this key was my only possession in the world as well as soon going to unlock my future. Opened the door and went up the 3rd floor. But at the same time I came aware that Antichrist had changed the lock to the apartment, I noticed a piece of paper on the door.

I used to love you so.
Now, fuck off Dick!

The expression; looking down the barrel of a gun, now comes in handy. Because as I shouted "Can we talk about it?" through the mailbox, that is what I found myself doing. Since no one trusts Antichrist less than I do, I surrendered and went down the staircase. You can't argue with Antichrist. Can't be trusted. I immediately recognized stuff from my past falling down from her balcony, forming a pile of memorabilia. Notebooks, records, my smashed Streetmaster, a superman costume, waders, a portable cassette recording device and a broken Boeing 747 model airliner, and more. Alright then. This was all I had, but since I suddenly was in the possession of a whole lot more than a minute ago I felt a little better than prior to the visit. I was freezing. I put on the superman costume, because Antichrist obviously didn't want to throw down my clothes. Too bad the original Superman evidently has tiny feet. Squeeeeezing them in there…! In some weird way the outfit felt very empowering. Invincible. There were voices singing inside my head.

"Don't you know I have a plan?"

"Na, na, na, na, na, na, na, naaaa!"

"Don't you know that I am Superman?"

"Na, na, na, na, na, naaaa!"

I picked up the model plane. There were people in there. I was in there. In the cockpit. It's my plane. I'm the captain. Uniform and shades. Now I'm walking in slow motion out of the hangar to my 747. Rock n' roll blasting from an indefensible large boom box on my shoulder. Me first. The crew accompanies in a triangular formation behind. I'm beautiful. We march in rhythm towards the airliner. 10 000 people are standing behind fences screaming and crying their eyes out for me. So much love. Suckers! I have the sun in my eyes, but that's okay because that's my only worry in the world right now. I take a sip of whisky right from an Isabella's Islay Whisky bottle. And another one. You know, I'm a a star. The crowd goes "Super duper! Super duper", in a low pitch chant.

I look up at Antichrist's balcony. I let her know it from the bottom of my lungs.

"Megastar!!!"

I collected the remains of a life long gone and was on my way to stardom.

/Dick

April 23rd 2022, Rehearsal basement

I didn't tell you about the second key. The key to the basement where I used to meet up with the band. It was on the same keychain as the one to Antichrist's apartment. I live here now. From time to time I go to the corner and do as Mr Reed and wait for my man. He was right on the aspect of time; he's always late. Wrong though in terms of the economic part. The drugs I purchase are not available for the amount of 26 dollars or less. Upholding an acceptable living standard has certainly become very costly for the average substance addicted citizen. The solution must be either committing to a life of crime, or rock n' roll superstar world domination. I choose a bit of both. Plan to make a hit. A timeless piece of rock that is, not a murder.

The portable cassette recording device is functioning at an acceptable level, surprisingly. Also, I managed to glue my guitar together and found new strings in the basement. No need to get new gear for the pre-production, but at some point will I need to get access to a real recording studio. I have one in mind which doesn't have an alarm system.

/Dick

April 29th 2022

Sometimes I'm alone. Other times it's a crowd. I can tell it's all in my head because I'm doing all the talking. At least, I know what everyone is gonna say right before they say it. So, I go first and they repeat after me. I'm like the high priest commanding the masses. They chant my words giving me the power to levitate. Completely normal for this type of song writing process. Inspiration comes like an ever flowing stream. Oh! That's an album title that is a strong candidate for the top ten list. *Like an Ever Flowing Stream.* Anyway, a stream of consciousness. So much to tell. Whatever I write is materializing. Ceiling. Wall. Radiator. Pills. Spider. Hand. Eating spider. Mouth. Vomit. Smell of vomit. Fingers playing. Ears listening.

Pressing REC now.

"Shut up!!!"

/Dick

3rd Levitation – Light Speed Centipede

I'm beautiful and loved I can't help that you hate yourself come closer you wanna jump my bones watch me levitate dead weight primate got it pretty sweet sweet like sugar sweet love and also and in particularly other matters pass me that mirror I wanna watch myself do the locomotion stamina it's all stamina if you wanna get to the top that's where I live the top rooftop jump jump all dressed up like hell speaking of hell is it there your hell or is it not in any case it's a lot of talking about that place leave me be come closer to your death it's me it's we it's a bee toodiloo pla pla plouw surely at the pinnacle of modern lyrics Nobel prize of literature material for sure no doubt little pig little wig as they say and the wolf comes along after it's all over and whines about his rights and how offended he is and those in favor say aye and that's that time to get to the last chorus 'cause I can't hold back any longer must sing the chorus one more time can't do it it's too painful and the blood is making a puddle on the carpet and it's filled with little versions of Christ little God and me as the spirit animal all the power and all the glory some animals breathe through their asses and I'm one of those I think it's not as bad as you might expect light speed centipede I'm all the God you need deep fried

pesticide let's get crucified and the stadium is boiling for
me through thunderstorm and heavy rain chanting for
me all the power and all the glory and all the copyrights
in perpetuity and you know it's all about Dick.

/Dick

Quite a decent party. I levitated and eventually evolved into the light speed centipede. I'm clearly all the God you need. But the Father is nothing without the Son. That's me too. Together we evoked the Spirit and then all three helped in nailing my hand to a speaker cabinet to truly complete the reenactment. Hurts like hell now, but when you party through the night with good friends – might have been daytime, who knows – everything is possible. And a little blood just tightens the friendship.

For further inspiration I feel an urge for more everyday human contact. It's time to get to work, so to speak. I think I'll go to the office tomorrow. Pay a visit to the real world. I bet you didn't think I have employment. I'll explain later.
Gonna prepare thoroughly.

"Hand me that zip lock bag and a razor blade, man."
"Certainly, Sir! And the mirror?"
"Obviously, Jeeves!"
"Should I put on some mood setting tune on the turntable for you, Sir?"
"Yes, please."

”*British Steel* coming right up, Sir.”

”Fire up the amp real good, Jeeves! Don’t spare my ears!”

”Of course, Sir. Is that alright for you?”

”Louder, motherfucker!”

”Certainly. Sir!”

Oh Rob, what a God you are.

/Dick

May 2nd 2022

I have a part time job at telemarketing company that is run by an old friend from high school. I didn't attend school for very long, but I managed to get him in debt and addicted to crack there for a while. I used to pick on him. Then we laughed. I laughed at him and he laughed because I did. So close friends. Years later I sort of forced him to employ me since I lied in court, telling the judge I had a job. Because I had work, I didn't get sentenced to jail. For reasons involving mild threats of going public with his history of substance abuse, my friend helped me out. I showed up for work occasionally. My sales were through the roof! No, seriously, I just hung out playing office, talking incoherently to random elderly people on the phone and giving my colleagues a hard time focusing on their tasks.

So I got up early and went outside for the first time in days. As I...wait! Something is not right. Be right back.

/Dick

”I EAT PEOPLE!”

”Really…?”

”Yeah!”

”Why this dramatic whispering?”

4th Achievement – Necessary Key Employee

Okay. So, I have to keep it down 'cause they might be listening in.

"Am I saying this out loud?"

"No, continue."

I can't tell who these dark figures are, but it's without a doubt; their intentions are not friendly. I can hear them mumbling through the walls. They think I don't know. Think they are real clever. But I'm on to them. Need to stay awake though. That's the only defense I have. The ones who sleep get taken away to a top secret international military base. Sedated for years and mentally altered by seven feet tall scientists in crimson robes and get injected with the blood of cute little rabbits. Soooo soft little furs…!

"Gonna get a rabbit's foot in my belt!"

"Shut it!"

This is of course just a hypothesis, but clearly within reasonable doubt. I might have experienced this already, I'm not sure. Since I lack recollection of big chunks of my life, I think it's a possibility. I'm so tired right now. My eyes are itching.

Anyway, I went to work, just acting all normal. Sippin' coffee and chattin' with the boys. I can tell they look up to me and consider me a valuable coworker. A necessary key employee who contributes important knowledge and insights that make the organization thrive. They're so lucky to have me. My role at the workplace is not limited to specific tasks, but rather free floating, allowing me to experiment and research. My main focus is to work on strategy and sustainability in sales towards key account customers as well as strengthening the team's collaborating skills through inclusion, validation reports and quality certificates. It's so much fun.

So, I was working on a solution to project small objects across the cubical landscape when the boss came over, wondered where I'd been and as a paper clip bounced off his large forehead, he asked me to step into his office. The others smiled and gave me encouraging little nods as I got up and followed him through the corridor. He sank down in his Chief Executive Officer appropriate leather chair with a creak and stroke his bald spot repeatedly with his ever moist hands. He glanced at me and immediately placed his attention elsewhere. On a mug of pencils. There was a picture of his ugly, obese children on it. They wore enormous best-dad-in-the-world home knitted pullovers. I could taste stomach acid.

"Hey buddy…", he started. I said nothing. Just kept thinking of my latest invention.

"You know we're grateful for all you've done for the company".

I thought of how to get the precise amount of energy behind the ammunition, transferring enough energy to the projectile to make it travel a path in such a curve that I from my cubical could reach the furthest target in the perimeter. That's the boss' office.

He was breathing heavily.

"It's time you think about your future."

And I thought about my future. I saw myself on stage, arms outstretched as nailed to an invisible cross. The enormous soaking wet audience grasping for air in the burning night. One more time, one more time! Megastar!

The boss coughed and cleared his throat. I snapped out of it.

"Q4 was slow, so we got to, you know…"

A forced laugh followed as he got up and put his jacket on.

"Well, I'm sure you see the implication", he said halfway out in the hallway and then he was gone. As he gave the impression of having said what was to be said, I left the room. Wondering what he meant, I couldn't help myself thinking of promotion and that this was my time to move up in the organization and definitely start to bring home some serious dough. Maybe he's retiring? Yeah, surely he has started the process of replacing himself. I'm the new boss! Makes sense. I carried on with my tasks at hand, but soon felt the urge of trying out my new office. I went back and as my first executive decision I decided to smash the nauseating picture mug against the furthest wall. I sat down. That creaking sound again. Leaned back and closed my eyes. At this point in time it's going real well for me, I think. Got my own office, head of a prospering business and a nice backward tilt. The perfect moment to take a little nap before I make some important changes to the company structure. As a newly appointed executive it's always of utmost importance to show the people on the floor some action, like laying off some dead weight, charging ridiculously for the coffee, public corporal punishment or promoting annoying fuckers to made up bullshit positions far away from vital functions. There can be no doubt that I am a bad ass leader. A little fear will do the trick. No one will feel safe under my supervision. I know they hate me, which is good to some extent, but they have to fear me just enough to never even thinking of challenging my authority. I have to secretly get a spy out there. I will employ a mercenary without any connection to the others who's loyalty I never have to question. Strategy 101. I could write an instructional manual on this shit! Being a total Dick, I would call it.

"Hey buddy! What the hell are you still doing here?"

A bit startled, I jumped back into the real world. Suddenly uncertain of what to think of the current situation.

"I'm planning for the future…?", I said in a tone of voice not revealing if I was resolute or posing a question. It's vital to always use the right amount of ruler techniques in every situation. In this case creating uncertainty. Giving a straight answer showing seriousness and determination for what to come, but with a slight ritardano, smoothly ending on an up note. This adds, if done right, confusion. Determination, curiosity and positiveness, yet leaving your counterpart unsure of your intentions. Planting thoughts like: Are we friends or enemies? Can I take him down if I have to? To ask questions is in itself a great technique for sucking up to superiors. It appeals to their ego and they feel important when they have to explain. Remember to ask a lot of questions; even if you know the answer. In this situation I didn't know what was coming, though.

"Get your stupid ass out of my chair!" All of a sudden he sounded like a boss. I was confused.

"What the hell are you talking about?!", I shouted. Best to fight fire with fire. A moment of silence. Behind the person that was clearly still the CEO of this shit hole stood the rest of the staff. One of them, whom I use to call Mrs Lobotomy because she's the wife of the boss, was holding a box containing my personal belongings. To bad I didn't hold the CEO position long enough to promote her to parking lot supervisor. Obviously I was let go and instantly got pretty upset. I cope poorly with rejection and afterwards I tend to repress the memories of my actions during outbreaks. So, some things were surely said and some body parts were probably shown just to make a point that felt relevant at the time. Left my keys and got my last paycheck at the reception before I walked out the door. Suckers.

/Dick

**Heeey dick
found yo dairy! U sucka lil girlie
muthafakka! don get haf o tis yo
brains soooo todal shiiiiiid!
Don tell bout us!
Yo be warned**

Poopie

Alright… I'll just leave that one there and move on. He's such a pain in the ass. Never miss him when he's gone. Always comes back though. I've known him since I lived in London. Would love to get rid of him but I can't. Most annoying ever. But harmless. I think…
I will have to keep the notebook with me at all times. This can never happen again.

I've lost one of my demo tapes. Is it stolen…? I feel unsafe.

/Dick

May 4th 2022, Outside

I'm hiding in the bushes behind the office building's staff entrance. I'm waiting for darkness. Seems it won't come any time soon. My last ever paycheck, corresponded to nine gallons of gas which I transported in an inflatable children's bath basin on a mail-cart I found behind the gas station. I brought my Streetmaster, the notebook, matches, some weed and the gasoline, obviously. If I had known it was springtime, I would have come later. Now it's a long wait getting into the right mood. That's the sun setting. Remember; gasoline is a poor substitute for sunblock. Smells nice though comparing to some minutes ago when the garbage truck was here. All is relative. I need to take a shower. Bad.

/Dick

May 4th 2022, Inside

I'm taking a little break. Challenging myself to get together a couple of chords and get the fingerpicking just right for this new song I'm writing. My God, they will call me a legend forever after I'm done with this life! Trying to calculate the perfect hit, X, using this progression:

$$X = \frac{Asus2\ Am\ Asus\ Am7/G\ D7/F\#\ D6/F\#\ Dm6/F\ D6sus/G}{Asus2\ Am\ Asus\ Bm7\ C6\ Bsus\ B}$$

I'm back in the Chief Executive Officer appropriate leather chair with a creak. The guitar doesn't really fit between the armrests. Everything is just normal around the office, with the slight addition of smoke and some burning cubicles. I got blisters on my fingertips from playing. Oval shaped and blood filled. I chew on them. Stings. Strings. Things. Rings of blood on the floor. Perfect circles. I taste blood.

"Come on! Finish the song now."
"Leave me alone, then!"

/Dick

5th Strike – No Juice For Me

The first time I burned something to the ground I was like fourteen, at what time in every young man's life matches and flammable liquids are an exciting addition to the hard times puberty can bring. The psychiatrist later told me that it had something to do with sexual awakening and the suppression of it. Or was it the other way around…? Anyway, I had stolen six gallons of diesel from a construction site which I poured out in the school yard. It was surprisingly hard to set fire to, but eventually my efforts paid off. A sea of burning $C_{12}H_{23}$ raged before me. Sweet. But a sea of burning diesel is very slippery, which I learned the hard way when I panicked and tried to jump on the flames to put them out. Had to roll around in the playground gravel for a while to save myself. But I couldn't stop the fire from spreading to the nearest building. The school cafeteria elimination was a popular incident though, because the kids hated the food and now the school had to bring in today's special type of dishes from the local diners. Got suspended and started to rob liquor stores instead, selling the booze to my class mates. This is when I got my tattoo. Flashes, just like my name and my mind. Would actually be a good idea for a band logotype. Haven't really burned something down since and come to think of it – I did make my sexual debut some time after the cafeteria incident. What do you know!?

This time it's more personal. I was told they had no use for me. That will be the name of the song. *No use for me.* Or it could be *No juice for me*, maybe? That's it. So, I feel humiliated and that feeling calls for vengeance. If I have nothing, they can't either. After spending hours in the bushes, I broke in and soaked the place in gas. Lit it up with a smile on my face. Okay, so I'm jumping back and forth here, but I think I got all important information through. You get the picture. I have a bad cough. Can't concentrate. Want to sleep. There's my guitar. Burning. Man, what a disappointing sight… The strings snap. One by one. Ping…twang…plop…
"Didn't like it anyway. No strings attached, so to speak."
"Hey, that's funny!"
It's getting hotter than hell. I have trouble breathing. Getting second thoughts now. Maybe I can put it out. Or maybe not… Better move out.

/Dick

I didn't write that shit. Just need to let you know. I have some lower standards, you know.

I won't take it out though, because I want to provide some insights into how my mind is, or in this case, isn't functioning as expected. I know I'm a freak. But also a genius. And good looking as fuck.

/Dick

May 4th 2022, The reception

Got to the reception. Crawling on the floor. Poor vision. The smoke is thick. Having serious second thoughts about this. Almost out. In bad condition. Can hardly breathe. Coughing like the lungs are gonna burst. I'm out of tears. Don't know to what degree, but my skin burns like hell!
Pain.

Hurts.

Pain hurts.

In pain!

Out…

Out…

Crawling…   …out…

…it's…

<u>Dear patient!</u>

My name is Miguel and I work as a janitor at the hospital. I actually have a PhD in both medicine and microbiology, but since I'm an immigrant I sweep floors and take out the garbage here. If you don't remember, you told me to help you write down some things in your notebook. It was not easy to follow your rambling, but I did my best. Happy to help. This is your words:

6th Confession. Nothing less than magic. I know it's a dream. I am disfigured. I'm alone. Center stage. Angry audience. Knock, knock. I forgot. Such a bore. Expecting more. Taking my clothes off. Playing the guitar. Everyone is angry. They want a magic trick. I play a sweet solo on my Stratocaster.
They like it. Love me. They are looking for this. Thunderstorm, clowns, monkeys, fighting, surfing, dead people arise. They hate me. I hate them. You bunch of losers. Fuck you.

Feel better soon!

/M

Act 2, Scene 76 – Family breakfast

Fade from black. Family eating breakfast.

"We woke up happy!"

"Stop it!"

"Let us tell the story! You're too slow and you're remembering it wrong!"

"No, I'm not, shut the fuck up!"

"When primates like gorillas are studied by scientists…"

"Shut up"!

"I'm unable to feel empathy. I don't know what it means."

"Really? I'm lacking mind's eye. Aphantasia, you know."

"I know what happened!"

"Uhhh, Mr Important is showing off again."

"Am not!"

"Too!"

"Get out of here! Everybody! You too!"

"Just trying to help."

"I'm the teacher's pet, boohoo."

"Dad, can I go play with myself?"

"Sure, son, just go easy on your spinal cord."

"A little pee can come a long way when aiming for the stars."

”How are you hanging in there? With the medication and the therapy?”

”Well, it's a relief to finally have someone to talk to but the pills aren't working.”

”*I'm* not working! I got fired!”

”Fire!”

”The flames of the end!”

”You could self-medicate instead! I know a guy that…”

”Shut the fuck up! You wanna hear this or what??”

Sorry…just…”

”Alright…? Alright.”

”Start then…!”

”I will, listen up. Shh… I had just begun to slowly wake up and was just barely aware of distant sounds and movements.”

Fade to hospital exterior. Voice-over continues.
Cut to close-up on patient in hospital bed.

7th Escape – Barefoot On The Run

So, I woke up in the intensive care unit. I could tell my awakening was unexpected, because the nurses and doctors started to run around and machines went ping, ping, ping. Full action. Holy mother, what a pain! I tried to scream, but the outcome was just a hissing sound, like a horror movie drone. I got a substantial injection of what I of course recognized as morphine. Relief. I let my head fall. Staring, empty eyed. To my right was a wardrobe with the door left open. The door was also a mirror facing me. I felt an instant chill to the bones when realizing that the terrifying face staring back was mine. That heap of cold cuts could not charm anyone. Not even Antichrist. It was me, but at the same time it wasn't. I could see that the figure tried to reach out to me. I could see his pain. I could feel it.

"We're not so different", I tried to say. He said it back in the same way. Felt true connection.

First I had a hard time to recollect why I had been hospitalized. Took days to sort it out. Since I had been out for over two weeks I had sort of left the field wide open for other residents of my mind to wander about unattended. They still do. It's a constant chattering about petty things. Imagine brainstorming with ten idiots, but firstly they are all inside your head, secondly they never stop and thirdly everyone of them has their own topic to discuss. They like to listen to my stories though. Then they keep calm.

"You're right! I'm like suuuuuper caaaaalm right now!"

"Shut up, let him tell the story!"

"Shhh…"

Anyway, where was I…? Right. I tried to pick up where I left off and it was actually a big help when I soon got a lot of visits by the police. I of course didn't answer any questions, but I could figure out pretty much what had happened just by hearing them. So every time I listened to what they said and then pretended to doze off. Oh, that's right. I was cuffed to the bed.

So, the resent events in conclusion; the headquarters of the telemarketing company owned by Mr and Mrs Lobotomy had gone up in flames. Turned out it wasn't a particularly prosperous business after all. It wasn't just Q4 that had been slow. Every important number in the books were red way back and since the company went bankrupt on the same day as the fire, Mr and Mrs Lobotomy had been taken into custody, accused of fraud and arson. I was believed to be an accomplice.

"I want to be an accomplice too!"

"Yes my son."

"Father…?"

"Go to your room! There will be no dessert for you!"

The doctors rounds gave me some more information. They went on and on like:

> The patient is a caucasian male. Age between 35 and 50. Identity unknown. Malnourished. Slight fever. Severe burns in the upper extremities. Cause of burn followed by flame. Total body surface area burn (TBSA) over 20%. Debridement followed by skin grafting done last Tuesday. Facial appearance prior to incident unknown. Reconstructive surgery based on assumptions successfully performed. Analgesics prescribed. Conscious at times. Incoherent. Threats have been made. Authorities informed.

The above is maybe not completely accurate. I left out everything I didn't understand; figures and percentages of various abbreviations and such.

I was nearly dying. Of boredom that is.

"We're here for you!"

"I know."

Paradox of the day; what keeps me sane are the voices in my head. They want to come out and play. I'm too weak.

"You can do it!"

"Yes I can!"

"You're disgusting!"

"What a man!"

"Pleased to meet you!"

"We don't care for little bitches!

"Alright shut the fuck up now! That last couple of phrases are actually pretty decent, I'll use them for the second verse, alright? Keep it down and I'll maybe let you all do the background singing, okay?"

"I wanna play the tambourine, please…!"

"The djembe can produce a wide variety of sounds, making it an extremely versatile drum, I've been told. I can play that!"

"Sure you can."

"Yeah right, haha!"

Back to the hospital bed now! It was dark outside the windows and seemed to be completely still. With a little encouraging support from you all I managed to gather strength enough to break the bed and was soon finding myself having difficulties standing up. Snuck out to the nurse's office, broke a glass cabinet and started to consume various pills. Sweet Lord what a trip. No pain. And also no time to lose. I decided to let the fire alarm go off, creating just the right amount of chaos to make a run for it.

I'm a pretty decent runner. Was always the fastest kid. Considered to be somewhat of a prodigy. A promise for the future for sure. And they were right. Back in -96 at the summer Olympic Games in Atlanta I won the 400m hurdles gold medal. They actually let me out of prison just to let me compete. So incredibly stupid to just give away a piece of fuckin' gold to a junkie inmate! Suckers! Pickin' a lock. Lickin' a sock. Stickin' a knock. Plickin' a flock.

"Make us prouder!"
"Take a stand!"
"We're getting louder!"
"I'm in command!"
Yes, I'm with you. You're with me. I'll do anything. I can see the door to freedom now. Heavy breathing. The sun. No, a lamp. Security guard! No, it's an elderly woman with a hatchet! Out! Out of the ER! Firetrucks! Helmets on heads! Heads on firemen. Firemen on ladders. Ladders on trucks. Trucks on wheels. Wheels on heels on seals.
"Out of the ER, barefoot on the run!"
"Get your shit together!"
"We're in control!"

I can do whatever!
Rock n' roll!

/Dick

June 11th 2022

Rumor has, I wouldn't get picked for running any long distance international championships at this point. I'm off the team. I seem oddly out of shape. Must be the hospital liquid food. Just gonna make a quick stop to catch my breath and get some things down on paper before I forget.

I came to think of tennis. Maybe because my balls hurt. More precise, I thought of the teaching of the technique behind this game. My mother's name was Leni Bolthausen. She was a dutch seasonal working tennis instructor at a top notch gated community retreat in Malaga. This top notch gated community retreat in Malaga is also where my father, Richard Stunningham Jr. spent the summers of his youth, away from the Liebefeld Steinhölzli state school in Köniz, and away from the family Stunningham's castle in Cornwall. The tennis court of the top notch gated community retreat in Malaga is the location of my creation. This particular summer in -74 was also the summer my father was to be married to some half-royalty and this particular afternoon, the close to 300 guests were starting to arrive. My father was a complete fuck up, but rich, which let him do whatever he wanted and act like a total ass in every situation, never considering any consequences. But he was also almost as good looking as me and a real smooth talker. So, after turning up late and intoxicated for his tennis lesson and after a few advices on how to improve his top spins and smashes, his instructor, a.k.a. my mother, was lured into the net which also served as a convenient thing to hold on to when leaning forward. My mother was fired on the spot by the retreat manager and the wedding was suddenly mysteriously postponed, due to *unforseen circumstances*, leaving the guests quite confused. My father was some days later found deceased after a self inflicted deliberate opiate overdose. Presumably, the reason was the effect of a blackmail situation, as a paparazzi had immortalized the creation of me and threatened to publish the photos in The Sun. Since the publication of those photos would have made my grandfather Richard Stunningham Sr. cut my father Richard Stunningham Jr. off as heir and certainly also would have pissed off the bride to be, my father found himself out of options. Death before humiliation.

The above information is the pretty solid fruit of my own investigational efforts. Had to find out for myself since I never knew my mother. She gave birth to me eight months later in the kitchen garden of a convent in southern France, where she resided until she died.

Aided by the nuns, she managed to get me out. There was a lot of blood and screaming. A bit too much blood actually. Before her passing she named me after my father and asked the abbess to take care of me. Given away barely alive.

There's a lot more there. The whole journey from being an innocent child thrown out by the abbess…
"Enfant maléfique, tu es possédé par des démons ! Disparaître !"
 …to the day I first entered the madhouse.
"Hej, Richard. Jag förstår att du inte mått så bra på sistone. Vi ska försöka hjälpa dig att bli frisk."

I'll dive in deeper into this story later if I feel like it.
Now I got to keep moving!
"Move it, fuckers!"
"Language!"
"Would you mind letting me pass…?"
"Better."

/Dick

8th Return – Crashin' Into The Night

The world is full of free stuff. Found an RV with the engine running. It's taking me out of the city on small dark roads. The trees are calling me home. I have to lay low for a while, but I also need to at least try to escape the voices. They're driving me insane. Only one channel is working on the radio. It's a nineties extreme metal music channel. I love that shit! The volume is maxed. *Mass appeal madness, Skin her alive, Beneath the remains, Corporal jigsore quandary, Stranger aeons, Birth of ignorance, Lack of comprehension.* Kick ass tunes! Death metal fills my head. And my mind. Truly beautiful! Shredding and growling and blastbeats. The aggression is so soothing for my restless fucked up mind. This is actually working. Death works! The voices are gone. I'm alone at last and the only thing in my head besides the music is my own thoughts. The others don't care much for blast beats and growling, I guess. It's something about the total brutality of the musical expression that appeals to me in a profound way. It's like when looking at art and there's something in a painting that is dead ugly and disturbing, but it's portrayed in a way that shows the underlying beauty of it. My mind is a string down tuned to B encountered by a buzz saw. Reminds me of when I first got tinnitus.

I was attending a show in -92. The band was Death and I was head banging like crazy in the front row. Chuck was so close. The closest I've been to a genius, myself excluded. His spit hanging from his mouth to the floor was showering my face. True dedication. Amazing technique. In even the shortest breaks in the guitar riffs, he muted the guitar throughout the whole show with his pinky crooked around the volume knob. Micro breaks. That's fuckin' skills! The levels at live shows back then were just insane and the public address systems were crap, especially at venues putting up shows featuring this kind of bands. It was somewhere in the last song, *Pull the plug,* that I started to get an ache in my ears and even down my neck and throat. Speaking of plugs; earplugs was of course out of the question. Totally lame.

"Hey!"

"What?"

"That's my only regret in life!"

"What?"

"Plug 'em in, kids! You'll thank me later!"

So, I became dizzy and just stood there, squeezed between the stage and some freaked out punks. I couldn't move though; I would never miss a second of this despite the overwhelming pain, now spreading down my chest. Simply a too important moment. Afterwards, when the pain had left me, I had a constant high pitch tone in my head. I still have it. The more silent the surroundings are, the stronger it sounds. Trying not to think about it is the only thing that helps. And not thinking is my Achilles heel, as you might have noticed.

I need to get as far away from civilization as possible. To be alone forever. I'm crashin' into the night.

/Dick

"You're doin' alright."
"Alright, now I feel like it."

Part I

Youth

Some version

Since I hate to repeat myself, I'll just pick up where I left off. Alright, just a brief recap then; southern France 1975, parents dead, residing in a convent. Since the convent was the home of women of many different nationalities, I picked up a lot of languages. That's the one good thing I got from that place. It's been easy to make my way through world, being able to mostly understand the native tongue of my surrounding, wherever that might have been.

It's a blur at first. Most memories are vague until my seventh year, but some things stand out as crystal clear. I had no doubt what so ever in the existence of God. I knew of nothing else. Might just have to do with the company I kept. Evil nuns mostly. I was constantly afraid of being sent to hell and I was often told that there was a great possibility that this might happen real soon. I believed I had a demon inside me which could control my mind and my actions and that I had let it in because of my weak faith. This demon was to be battled through flogging and praying. I have the scars to prove it. Whenever I said or did something that wasn't considered being up God's alley, I was sent to the abbess with a willow branch of my own choice to get correction until the branch broke. I bled a lot. I know she loved every second of these little meetings. She always smiled at me when I appeared in her office and while I took my shirt off she used to pour herself a glass of Malbec. Her warm and excited breath reeked of alcohol and pleasure. The corporal punishment was quite overwhelming at times. In hindsight I'm pretty sure that she saw a real threat in me and hence took the opportunity to give vent to her own self hatred. Remembrance of feeling wrongly accused. The growing animosity towards authorities. And the arising disappointment in Christ as I stared deep into his empty eyes. Hanging there nailed to the cross on the abbess' wall, unable to come to my aid. I felt like a caged animal. As a not so silent protest I sneaked down to the wine cellar and broke some bottles. Felt good. This was in -79 and that's when I got the tase for wine. Felt even better. A little numbness made the flogging easier to endure.

The most important and also the turning point for my me was my encounter with a priest who frequented the convent. I know what you're thinking, but it wasn't like that. He was my English teacher and he is the reason I can spell these words. He took interest in me and started to ask me questions about the abbess and the nuns. We became friends. At one point he showed me a tape recorder and asked if he could interview me. I thought it looked cool and was intrigued when he played back my voice. Then it happened. He rewinded and changed the tape. Pushed play. Holy mother! I was blown away. The sound coming out of that shitty cracked speaker and bounced between the stone walls was instantly my only religion. Jesus could go fuck himself. Later I learned that it was the opening track *Speed King* from *Deep Purple in Rock* from -70. Suddenly I had found my purpose in life. I wanted to sound like that. Bad. How was this sound created? What's a Stratocaster? You can scream your lungs out and people will pay good money to listen to it? I was filled with a feeling I never felt before. Happiness. I had a million questions. Few were answered at that point. Instead he surprisingly made it clear that there was no God and that the nuns were abusing me. There was another life out there for me. Seemed highly reasonable. He gave me new perspectives on life as I started to question everything I knew about the world. A spark was lit inside that soon evolved into a raging fire.

I remember our last conversation. He told me that he wasn't a priest and that he wouldn't come to visit me again. That he in fact was an undercover journalist digging into the fucked up conditions in the convent. I sure gave him some interesting insights which he thanked me for. The story was eventually published in the local paper. Even the Pope was upset. But by then I was long gone because no force in the world could hold me back anymore. I had a fire inside that needed more fuel. If I didn't feed it soon it would consume me instead. The journalist had offered to help me escape. He told me to pack my things and wait for darkness. And so I did. At midnight I heard a ridiculous little honk, that could only come from a French automobile. I ran down the stairs without a sound and out through the heavy gates. I spit at the door and shouted from the bottom of my lungs.

"Au diable Jésus !"

As the car door closed and I sank down in the uncomfortable seat, I felt years of agony slowly turning into sweet euphoria.

"Alright, let's get you the life you deserve."

We were off to London.

Back then it was easy to fake papers and travel unnoticed across borders. Hidden in the trunk of a -57 Citroën 2CV whiteout brakes, I came to Calais, crossed La Manche and was soon accommodated with a foster family in Chelsea. I have no memories or information of why I came to them, but I recon that the journalist had made the arrangements. Haven't seen him since. Anyway, it was a totally dysfunctional family with way too many kids with too many problems. My first question when I arrived was where I could find Deep Purple, but they just laughed and said they were disbanded. I was devastated, of course. My new siblings were mean little glue sniffing potheads. So I eventually tried to blend in and picked up the basics of these habits. Spent most of my time in the streets making my way as a quite talented pickpocket. Scored some quids, spent it on grass, slept, scored some quids, bought glue, slept… High life. Got in a lot of fights. Attended school occasionally just to assure that I didn't get expelled. This went on for a while but I also educated myself in the field of rock n' roll. There was a massive load of albums released, that I needed to get. So I manically consumed every record I could get my hands on, playing them day and night on an old turntable I exchanged for my foster father's watch. Couldn't get enough of those records. At ten years of age I stole my first Stratocaster and a Vox AC30 at a second hand store at Portobello road and began to learn the basics. How I loved the sound of it! Couldn't get enough of myself playing. Fingers bled, but I didn't care. As I heard that tone I was unable to feel pain. Soon I could handle it real well, my fingers didn't bleed anymore and I was even starting to write my own songs. Here I started to lose track of my mind for the first time. Didn't know what was happening around me. Didn't care. Kind of hypnotized myself in a haze of dreams and fantasies about rock n' roll. Always playing that guitar. Time went by unnoticed. Years. I was only there in the moment and nothing else was of any relevance. Just focused on the one thought; music. And drugs. I don't know why, but one day I kind of woke up. It was perfectly clear to me what was to be the purpose of my life. It was rock n' roll and all the things that come with it. The sex and the drugs, you know. The holy trinity. I mean; I had known that for years, but now it got serious. No time to lose anymore.

So, my mind was all set on leaving shitty London. It was cold and damp and I was suspended from school since some time. I had lived like a homeless thief since my experiment with fire that I already told you about and my goal was set on getting my ass to America. I had started to work on a plan and by -91 I put the wheels in motion. First; cut back on the drugs and get cash. So, I stole and sold off everything I could get my hands on and saved up as much as I could. Made a lot of enemies and technically I'm still in debt, I think. But so far, so good. To carry out the second, more intricate part of the plan I needed an easy victim. It took months to finally find the perfect one and I had almost given up, when my determination paid off. As I lurked in the shadows, the perfect moment suddenly presented itself. It played out something like this. Pretty evil shit, when you think about it.

The whole time I had my eyes on the target. As he walked towards the Nightliner I pretended to just happen to be in his way.

"Oh, sorry!"

"My bad!"

"Hey, great show but the way!"

"Thanks, kid!"

"Really love your tone!"

"Alright, thanks."

"I think you have problem with your tuning, though. The intonation is off."

"Get lost!"

"I can fix it way better."

"Yeah, sure."

"Sorry, don't mean to be a bother, it's hard to find good guitar techs."

"Go home to mommy, it's past bedtime."

"Just…I have a question, if that's okay…?"

"I have to get on the bus now, but thanks for coming."

"Just wondering if it's true…?"

"What? I really have to go."

"Oh, nothing then. Just what the singer said to the drummer. But never mind, bye!"

"What did that fucker say?"
"Never mind. Maybe I got it wrong."
"What!? Wait! Come back here!"
"Well…can I have a beer?"
"Said what?!"
"A beer?"
"No, what he said?"
"Oh, nothing really, just that thing about your girlfriend…"
"What the fuck? Spit it out!"
"Alright, he just asked him…"
"Who?!
"The drummer."
"Asked him what?!"
"That thing about your girlfriend."
"What about her?"
"Well she and the bassist and…"
"What!?"
"…and the singer and…
"And who?!"
"…and the merch guy…"
"You little piece of shit! What are you saying?!"
"Can I have a sip of your beer?!
"Here! Take it! What he fuck are you saying?!"
"Or maybe it was the guitar tech…?"
"I knew it! That fucking asshole! Johnny, get your ass over here!"

"Hey, man, what's up?"

"This time I'll fuckin kill you!!"

"What did I do?"

"Don't even try to deny it! I've seen how you look at her! I will fuck you up!"

"What?! Stop hitting me!"

"Let go of my guitar you shit hole fucker! You're out!"

"What? You're hurting me!"

"You've fuckin' touched my gear for the last time, motherfucker!"

"What is happening right now?"

"You're out of work, that's what! Get out of here, fucker!"

"Well, I quit! You can tune your fucking piece of shit guitar your self, asshole!"

"Suits me just perfectly! We will never speak again! Fuck off!"

"Fuck you too! Fuck all of you!"

"What's you name kid?"

"Dick. I'm Dick Stunbolt. I'm a guitar God."

"Really...?"

"Really."

"Well, Dick. Do you need work?"

"I already have work. I'm your new guitar tech."

As I jumped on that bus I left everything behind and entered life as I know it.

"You know it!"

As it wouldn't benefit anyone to reveal the name of the band in question, I won't. I can just say that it was a quite good up and coming American rock band which didn't survive long enough to get to the fame they might have deserved. I suspect that the numerous internal conflicts teared them apart. After their first European tour they kind of vanished. Their greatest accomplishment was the fact that they served as the first important stepping stone in my career in the world of rock n' roll. I went with them on the remainder of the tour, tuning guitars, carrying a shitload of gear, whispering rumors in the members' ears as well as getting all the drugs for them. In the end taking the guitarist's place as he became too strung out to get on stage. We left him behind after he fucked up a show in Oslo. As he was arrested for possession of illegal substances and striking a police officer, I conveniently stepped up and saved the tour from collapsing. Neat. I followed them to the States when it all was over. I was sixteen and the American immigration authorities took me into custody immediately at arrival. I had no papers. After a few weeks I was sent to a Philadelphia suburb, where I was to live with yet another fucked up foster family. And forced to attend Lincoln High.

”Dick, Dick, Dick…”
The Principal looked through some papers and pushed her thick glasses into the correct position. They started to slide down again. I was still holding the bloody paper tissues over my cracked eyebrow. I'd been in her office quite a few times already.
”Seems you failed again…” She looked at me as if she expected me to say something. I was quiet.
”Zero tolerance for drugs and violence. That's not your thing, is it?”
”I'm all for drugs, but as for the violence it was he…”
”Stop it! I don't want to hear it!”
”Alright…”
Just before I had gotten orders to visit the Principal's office, I had managed to get back a loan from the idiot cokehead quarterback. He cried as I broke his wrist. Now the football season was pretty much lost. Totally worth the eyebrow.
”I will make myself clear. You've been here for just over three weeks and I'm already out of patience. No more of this!”
”Alright…”
”You have nothing to say for yourself?”

What could I possibly say? That I had made the whole football team and all the cheerleaders high as kites and in debt to the local mobster drug dealers?

”Not really.”

”I can’t give you any more chances.”

”Fine.”

”You’re out, Dick.”

”Out how?”

”Like completely out.”

”No more school?”

”No more school.”

”That’s a relief! ’Cause I’ve got way better things to do!”

Just like that, my calendar was wiped clean. Free to do whatever I wanted. Sweet! It was time to put things in motion. Start a band and become a star, obviously. But first celebrate, of course. So, I kind of got stuck in the celebrating phase. And that wasn’t cheap. To finance my celebration I soon found myself working my way up as a hired gun, making collections and carrying out the dirty work needed to be done when you’re involved in organized crime. Loads of fun. I think? Wait. Or did I work at the hospital…? I don’t remember, honestly. I do however know that I told everyone I was a rockstar, because people started to ask how my band was coming along, but it didn’t really happen.

"Yeah, we're going on tour soon. Europe and South America"

"Cool."

Managed to celebrate a lot in the style of a rockstar, though. I lived like fifty-fifty on the street and in jail for some time. Some years really. Got my third strike in spring -94 and was sentenced to prison for burglary, theft and driving under influence. Got four years and took the opportunity to quit the drugs for a while. Worked out and read pretty much all books in the library. There's nothing of importance to share from that time. I got out in -98 and immediately started a band.

––––––––––

I'll stop here for now. The memories and my imagination are in conflict. The risk of making stuff up is too imminent. I think I already overstepped. I'm not sure. Sometimes when I read it back to myself I recognize these memories. Other times it just comes out as lies. I need help.

/Dick

June 12th 2022, Four on the floor

The vehicle's windshield is like a large tv-screen and I'm using the controls to play a game. It sounds like fun. But there's only emptiness inside. The feeling of having gotten away is like the feeling after winning a game. First it's the greatest! Then it's boring. What now? I have no purpose being on this route. Just like a top athlete winning the championship gold medal. Euphoria followed by a total void. Further more, I really never cared much for gaming or the whole culture of that world. Maybe because I always got so insanely angry trying to carry out any type of gaming activities. Fuck it! I need to turn back now! Whatever shitstorm is coming; it's mine! Okay, game on again. More fun now. Dodging highlights like a chicken race pro! Getting the high score! It's on the radio. They are cheering for me and calling me a hero. Wait! They're back…! And as much as I hate to admit it, it's suddenly clear. I need those fuckers. I need them to stay alive. After all; we all share a profound love for each other.

"All together now!"
"Rushin' out of the night!"
"They tell me I'm doin' alright."
"The sole survivors are my backseat drivers!"

I can see the city lights fading away as I move closer.
I'm almost out of gas. And drugs. The night is over.
The sun is taking over. Morning is coming. I'm
sweating like a pig. I have won this game, but the
struggle continues.

"I'm the king of delight!"
"I'm crashin' into the light!"

/Dick

”So…what now…?”

”Well, did I tell you about the second time I died?”

Part II

Death

And the afterlife

Because I'm always surrounded by both friends and enemies there is in every situation loads and loads of suggestions for what is to be my next move. The hard part is to choose wisely. Mostly I go for the dick moves, you know. The self destructive path is so much more instantly rewarding and always give life a touch of excitement. On the other hand I know I'll feel better in the end if I settle for the boring choices. Damn it! The solution to this is to go with the flow. Hence the ups and downs. I usually try to have as much fun as I possibly can until reach rock bottom. Then I take it slow for a while, sort my mind out and occasionally get my ass into rehab. Mostly during periods of deprivation of liberty. But being in prison trying to stay away from drugs doesn't necessarily mean that the load of mental issues are easing. Despite being clean I had one of my worst episodes in there. Figures from the inside started to materialize around me in the form of rabbits with human heads. My head. All looking like me. Small furry little shits hopping along everywhere I went. There were rabbits all over the place. Craving carrots. Constantly. It was so real that I decided to carve myself a shiv in the wood shop and started to go after them. To make them stop. I chased them around stabbing and waving like a windmill until I had almost drained myself of blood and was taken to the infirmary with some nasty cuts to the throat. When you aim pointy things at yourself it's hard to miss the target. I still see rabbits sometimes. But I try to jump on their heads instead. Like a video game. It's an easy game, so I don't lose my temper.

However, after bouncing in and out between freedom and various institutions for the lion's share of this life, I eventually came to a point where I was completely fucked in the head. This was some time before my second experience of dying and the year was perhaps 2016 or something like that.

I had without knowing made my way to the southern parts of Sweden and I barely knew who I was. My brain was a mushy, smudgy goo, floating around in a dark cloudy pool of thoughts, screams, drugs, fantasies, lyrics, whispers, delusions and rock n' roll. The last thing I recollect is the experience of entering naked into the underworld. The sacred hellish heaven of rock. Bells. Choirs. Chanting. And a huge organ playing Bach's *Toccata and Fugue in D minor* backwards. I never touched the floor. Blood was running up the walls creating a boiling pond below the ceiling. Blood drenched arms filled with track marks stretched down, trying to reach me. The sounds of nameless bodies grasping for air. Burning stone walls. Incredible heat. Fumes of death filled my lungs. And suddenly Satan stood before me, smiling and spreading his wings.

I'm there right now. It's happening again. It's taking place forever. This event is eternal. The sound of an earthquake roaring at deafening level. Everything around me shaking and crumbling. Satan takes a deep breath. Filling his lungs with fire and fumes and debris. Eyes of flames screaming out the collective pain of humanity's ancient sorrows. He looks at me. I'm petrified. He points his sharp dirty index finger nail at my hard pounding heart. He will speak to me now. My chest is about to break. I lose my sight.

"Take me…!" I whisper. "Take me home…!"

Everything stops. Sound ceases to exist. Time dies. Nothing moves.

"Excuse me, Sir. We're closing now. You're not supposed to be here. Can I help you?" he says in a somewhat hesitant mild tone with a Swedish accent.

I couldn't cope at all. I expected him to say something completely different. That's the thing with that guy; he can't be trusted even with the simplest tasks. You never know what you'll get. I felt disappointment. And pain. Still in pain. There was a headache so overwhelming that I nearly fainted. And then I must have done just that. Blackout. The end. Fin.

I was found dead at the feet of Finn the Giant. A stone sculpture in the crypt of the Lund Cathedral. Cardiopulmonary resuscitation was successfully carried out by the paramedics.

So there you have it; the passion of the Dick. Resurrected in the third minute. Praise the Lord of Darkness! Since I'm now alive for the third time I think it's safe to say I'm a greater miracle than Christ. Sucker! Best of all; this time I didn't have to pay for the resurrection.

So far there's little or no evidence what so ever to support the hypothesis that I will at some point die. Eternal life, on the other hand, is a possibility that has lately come to seem more than likely. If I die and come back to life again I will consider it a proven undeniable fact. If I just believe in myself there's no stopping me.

When I came to, I was dressed all in white. Everything was white. Even the iron bars covering the windows. They talked soothingly and nicely to me from outside my hazed tunnel vision. Felt like some Roman Catholic heavenly type of scenery. After some time my mind started to sharpen. The environment started to seem more like light grayish or off-white. My doctor was quite impressed with me. He had never treated a patient in a worse condition that actually got to live. I guess I'm a living dead. We talked a lot. I told a whole bunch of anecdotes from my previous life with various amounts of truth to them. This is when I started to write for real. An unstoppable flood of words just came out of the pencil, forming the most wonderful combinations of unexpected phrases melting together in front of me. I could just pick any letters and let them out to play until they gathered in organized smaller or larger groups after one another. Heavenly lyrics of angels. I thought. Have you ever read something that a mad person wrote by hand just after being brought back from death? It's not impressive. The spelling is all off and the grammar is a lawless country. I won't have it! As I got better I burned my first notebook in disgust with myself and rewrote everything. Then I burned that one too because the words came out in the same way. The third time I was about to burn my notebook I couldn't find it. I looked everywhere. Nightstand, bed, floor. Nightstand, bed, floor. The fuck…? That were the only places it could be. Nightstand, bed, floor… Suddenly I knew. It didn't exist. It was all in my mind. There had never been any notebooks at all. I realized that people in my situation do not get access to pencils or any sharp objects. There's also rules like that regarding matches. I thought is was a good thing that I at least had my guitar. But since I had clearly snapped out of some dreamy state I suddenly knew that the guitar didn't exist either. I felt a tiny thread of panic exponentially growing into a lead filled missile submarine sinking to the bottom of the Mariana Trench. Every sorrow I ever felt squeezed my chest into a gravitational singularity. I was nothing. Obliterated. Then the nurse came with my pills. She had forgot.

"Open up…all's fine. That's right. No need to get upset. There…and swallow. Good! I think the rain has stopped. This weekend the weather is going to get better. You can sit in the park with your friends. I'll even bring out the radio. Alright?"

I nodded slowly and felt my mouth being wiped. My mind turned back into sludge. The submarine was being salvaged.

The next day I burned my notebook again and practiced some of my songs on the guitar. I bought a new notebook and a pencil sharpener at the airport and began to write down what I believed to be some of my best work yet.

The story was about me and the singer from a punk band I played with. We were just hanging out. Low on cash, we had a brainstorm discussion trying to solve our monetary issue. We ended up printing posters which we put up all over town.

EASYKILL
We off all kinds
of old and sick pets.
$50 – cash only
555-K1LLM3N0W

Below was a bad drawn picture of a tombstone and a cat with crosses for eyes. Simple plan. Collect the pet and the cash. Release the pet in the woods. All posters were teared down immediately. No one called. End of story.

I don't know when this happened. But I know it was before I worked at the hospital. Logistics. Collecting garbage filled with shit and blood as well as driving the dead to the overfilled walk-in refrigerators in the morgue basement. There were fat transparent lazy flies making their way around the bodies. The nauseating smell was thick and sweet, especially on Sunday nights, because the pathologists didn't work on weekends. By then the residents were forced to share bunks, placed on top of each other. They couldn't care less. Their alive relatives might just have objected if they had known though. Mostly I moved around in the endless culverts plundering the little ridiculous food trains driven by old pale gray haired men who never spoke. Zombie train drivers feeding on cold boiled potato leftovers. The lack of vitamin D can slowly break anyone.

"Richard…?"
"…!"
"Do you think of me sometimes?"
"No."
"Why?"
"I can't remember. Maybe."
"Do you want to remember?"
"I'm not sure. You're not real."
"But I am. You know I am."
"Well…"

"What?"

"I don't need you anymore."

"Are you sure?"

"I'm sure."

"We had such good times together."

"Yeah, I know!"

"Well…? Can I come back and visit sometime?"

"I'm busy…I'd rather not…"

"I'm the only one who understands you, right? You once told me that."

"I wasn't thinking clear, you know…"

"Of course. I understand. It's just…"

"What?"

"Why would you throw it all away…I'm the best you ever had."

"Stop it! You're fucking up my head!"

"Yes I am. That's what I do. And you love me for it."

"Goddamn it!"

"Your desire are the same. No one can change that. You had me. And now I own you. Until death."

"Leave me alone! I don't need you!"

"You shouldn't lie to yourself, Richard."

"It's not a lie!"

"Define truth then."

"The truth is…"

"What?"

"I…"

"Hard, huh?"

"The truth is, every time we meet, something inside me breaks."

"Maybe that thing needs to be broken…?"

"What…?"

"It's an inner war raging and I'm on your side. I'm your champion. The enemy needs to be taken down. We'll fight the pain together."

"You're pure fuckin' evil!"

"You and I know what's true and pure. Together we're invincible. We'll become untouchable. Painless."

"Please stop talking. Leave me alone, please…"

"Alright. You're maybe not as strong as I thought. Take care of yourself, baby. I will soon visit you again and stay longer."

"Please…don't!"

"See you soon, my love."

"I fuckin' hate you. So much!"

She's gone. For now. Her name is Heroin. I do love her. But it's complicated.

———————

June 13th 2022

ow it's time to ask ourselves some relevant questions. It is also a rock n' roll quiz in the range easy to medium easy. We're all in the same team, so no prestige, alright? If you don't recognize the following you can go fuck yourself. Go!

"Where you goin' with that gun in your hand?"
"Is there anybody in there?"
"Where do we go now?"
"Will your tongue wag so much when I send you the bill?"
"What's goin' on?"
"What's love got to do with it?"
"Will you do the Fandango?"
"Who are you?"
"Don't you know that I am Superman?"

All these questions?

"Cut the crap! It's too easy! Let's go for brunch at the country club, I'm starving."

/Dick?

9th Miscalculation – Completely Ludicrous

The radio was silent. Like it had never made a sound. I climbed up through the 90 degrees tilted and smashed drivers window. The vehicle was totally wrecked and was placed on its side in the middle of a small pond by the green of the third hole of some posh country club's golf course. Ridiculously dressed overweighted business people and their up-sucking caddies ran around screaming. Like startled by something. It might just have been the unexpected appearance of an RV bouncing across the green, through a bunker and taking a leap like a gazelle into the pond.

"By the way…", I glanced at myself in the pond. The blood was dripping from my forehead. I looked badass.

"You look completely ludicrous with that Magnum 44."

I don't know where I got it, but it must have been a part of the RV's interior equipment. Waving casually with a firearm is a great way to get an open field. I completed the show for them by shouting incoherently.

"Gabbasharrassabilaaaahhhh, fuckers!"

In reflecting on and doing a fast evaluation of the club members living situations compared to my own, I got upset. Why these inequalities? I should start a foundation for my peers. Like a union for lunatics, maniacs and the deranged. I'd be the union boss, ensuring that the living standard for the less fortunate improves. Dramatically.

"What shall we do?"

"What you said!"

"Who will do it?"

"The Super Duper Megastar!"

"When will I do it?"

"This afternoon!"

"Alright, I'll check my calendar and see if there's an empty slot. Yes, I think I can squeeze it in there. Just between taking a leak and my three o'clock nap."

We will need some funds to get things started. Need to go to the bank and get a substantial loan. I hate banks. We hate banks. Therefor, I will not get a loan. But I will go to the bank. Since debt is not my thing I'll ensure they give me all the funds I need anyway. After all I've got a firearm I can wave around, making my intentions understood.

"I know I'm not supposed to go, But I do it anyway", singing to myself. For myself. About myself. All together!

I let myself know that this was by far the worst idea that I ever had.

"Mind your own business, fuckface!"

"Language!"

"Just trying to help…"

"Go help someone else!"

Taking that leak now.
Shake it.
Some more.
Shake it.

More?
Fuck it.

Let's make this happen!

/Dick

<u>The river</u>

― in which the protagonist sorts out the events that followed, shares his thoughts on fishing and has an unexpected encounter with a handsome traveller from abroad.

S ince I wrote last, there has been some development. It's been over two years now. So, about the time of my last notes, I went into a bank, slipped the teller a handwritten piece of paper expressing the demand to hand me a shitload of cash. Since I was under the influence of hallucinogen mushroom tea I was convinced I was carrying a Magnum 44 down my pants. Showing her the badly composed plywood pieces I pulled out didn't have the same impressive and intimidating effect as a proper firearm would have had, I think. Without the slightest change of face she calmly explained the situation.

"Hey, I have set off our silent alarm."

"Please stand back sir", a firm male voice said from behind me.

I froze.

"By the way", she looked at my gadget.

"You look completely ludicrous with that homemade piece of crap."

I definitely became the centre of attention. In a blink of an eye I was taken down and was suddenly facing the stone cold marble floor. Hard. All eyes on me. I don't mind that, after all I'm a star. But I'd rather like less attention at that sort of occurrence. The police was there within minutes and soon I was in custody. It felt like everything happened so fast. I know I was in court and got 18 months of detention. I freaked out because someone provoked me to make a run for it and in the riot that followed I accidentally kicked my lawyer in the nuts, resulting in another indictment. When in prison, they had decided that I was a threat to myself and sent me well medicated to solitary confinement. I can't tell for how long. Although I was in restraints, I wrote a few new songs in there. Seemed like eternity. But everything must come to an end, even eternity.

Without going into more details, I'm out again. Life is kind of like back to usual. Writing, playing, doing whatever drugs I feel like.

I like to go fly fishing this time of year. So a while ago I put my waders on and stepped out in the middle of a river. Like magic. As if the waders were haunted by the evil souls of a thousand trouts. Payback. Their ridiculous little mouth movements and empty eyes staring at the middle of my face. Not in my eyes. Between. Coming for me. I admit, it's a terrible thing to be out and about minding your own business and then maybe stopping for a snack and "Hey that looks yummy lets try that, okay I'll take a bite and"…BAM! You're hanging in a 20 inch steel hook from the mouth. It's pain so overwhelming that you might pass out. If you're lucky the hook went out your cheek. If not, that hook is sitting straight up in your brain. But it's nice to get out and about, embrace nature and breathe the fresh air.

It was right then I heard someone calling my name. I looked around, and saw a smiling face between the pines just behind me. The face was attached to a man in his forties. He was clearly happy.

"Mr Stunbolt?" It was a question, but I could tell he knew it to be a fact.

"Who wants to know?"

It's difficult to escape any situation when you're waist deep in a river.

"You're not very easy to find! But I thought if you could find me, I could find you."

His words made no sense but I could tell he was Danish. Since people with accents from all parts of the world at some point have told me to go fuck myself, I've become a wizard in the art of telling people's native tongue.

"You gave me this!" He held up a cassette tape in front of him, sounding 98 percent more as a Copenhagen resident than anything else.

There it is, I thought. The missing tape. I *gave* it to… him? Maybe…but why?

"I'm Claus…you know? We spoke on the phone…", he was somewhat hesitant. "I run Accelerator Records."

It's getting interesting. Have we met before? He acts like I at least know *of* him. A label boss. Certainly, it's not a major label, but never the less a label. I've been tracked down. That's disappointing, but since it's because of my music, it's alright, I guess.

He told me how the tape came in his possession. He found it taped to his window. Sounded likely. Seemed honest about wanting to release my stuff. Vinyl of course. He likes me. I'm likable. Gonna be a star. Megastar. He told me that he in some way came across some people who knew of me. According to them I had broke into a recording studio, worked through the night and then disappeared, leaving a lot of traces including drugs and master tapes. When talking to the dude with the studio, Claus had convinced him, with a little help from an unknown percentage deal, to let me come back to the studio, a little more sober, to re-mix and finish the recording. In some way I recognized that story. Had I heard it before? Did I already know this? I vaguely reminisce a recording session. I'm there right now? What's that…I can do it better…? Take 4?

"Take it from the top, Dick. I want you to go a semi-tone higher in the last bar, that'll do the trick."

I'm right there. Headphones on. In the studio singing booth. Got smokes and a bottle. Taking it from the top. Screaming my lungs out! The studio floor comes closer. I'm standing in the water. I'm on the river bed. I'm fishing. I'm moving fast. I'm in a tree. I'm the light speed centipede. I'm in the basement. I can't keep up with myself. So confusing. But fun!

Claus pulled out some papers. A record deal. I'm in the basement. Dark. I'm in waders?

"Read it through! It's a fair deal!" He tried to hand the papers to me through the iron gate.

"Give me a pen."

"Sorry! Wait…here…"

I figured, since I don't abide to any laws, it's perfectly safe for me to sign anything. No fucks to give. I put my signature on the dotted line. He was like a child on Christmas morning.

"Stand here! I want to take a picture of us together. And the contract! Let me just put the camera here… and…yes! Perfect! Stand still! I'll come around to this side…hold it…alright!"

Click!

He gave me his card, said thank you real nicely, take care, talk soon, don't hesitate to get in touch, send me the lyrics and the logo and I'll fix the rest, I'll talk to the studio, take care, Dick…and was on his way back through the forest.

I stepped back into the river.

"It's cold!"

"Shut up! You're the one who wanted to go swimming, for fucks sake!"

"I see fishes!"

"Nail me to the cross, mother. I need you to hurt me…"

"So dramatic! Always…!"

"Eat you fucking pancakes and maybe I let you come up from the water!"

"This isn't proper breakfast, it's the blood of Christ! Disgusting…"

My left hand fingers have started to have meaningless conversations with each other. The index finger is Mother and the middle finger is Father. The ring finger is silent. Weak and almost absent. The pinky is always complaining and sobbing. My thumb is doing most of the talking, throwing accusations at the others. He seems to be dead serious about the little finger being a traitor.

"Cut off Pinky, he's the traitor!"

"Shut up, Chubby!"

I ensure you all, I won't act on it. Typically, the one setting the tone in a group is some inconsiderate bastard thinking he's the know-it-all. So much better than all the others. More important. Deserves special treatment. He snaps at me. I ignore him.

By the way, I have stopped shaving. I swear, half the mayo I consume is trapped in my beard. Also, I'm thinking about moving out to the woods. Maybe I can live in a tree?

One with nature. All teeth and ticks and fleas.

Am I
a monster?

Conclusion

To be clear, my final remark is this; I have recorded a self titled album that will be released soon on vinyl. It's pure gold. That's why you can get it in gold if you want to. Black or gold – your choice. If you hold this book in your hand, just maybe you have bought it as well as the record at the merch stand at one of my shows. Maybe on the world tour. Who knows?

Better remind Claus to book a world tour as soon as possible.

"Claus! Get me a world tour! Now!"
"Yes, Master…!"

/Dick Stunbolt
November 22nd 2024

Me and Claus doing some paperwork.

Appendix C8

Fuck me! And just like that I have to leave you with the following depressing update:

You can for sure get more information elsewhere, but as for now the release of the vinyl is totally fucked. Turns out the vinyl pressing plant has gone bankrupt. I feel like doing every drug in the world at once. Sadly, I just have coffee, so I guess I'll have a pot of that. And gently weep. I guess I'm not gonna get the opportunity to show the world my greatness. Claus said the album is coming anyway on December 6th 2024, but only in digital form.

"What a load of crap!"
"Hey, with the screaming! Cool it man!"
"I want Mommy…!"
"I think it will turn out fine."
"Shut up! You don't know that!"
"Can we sue?"
"What about in the future when no one can access today's digital formats? No one will remember me…"
"Just thinking of it makes me sick!"
"It makes *you* sick? What about me…!?"

"I was to live forever. And now I'm practically dead."
"Dead forever! Yeah, cool!"
"Let's have a funeral instead of a release party!"
"I can do the Ave Maria!"
"Do you think you have the voice for it, though?"
"Open casket!!"
"Shut up, Chuck! For the love of Satan, Santa and Dick almighty!"
"I guess I'll just play along and see what happens."
"Yeah, that will do it, for sure…"
"Get the fuck out of here! Braindead morons!"
"Alright, talk to you later."
"Take care. Bye."
"Come on. We know when we're not wanted."
"Prick!"

I need to scream but I'm too exhausted. I'm done.

/Dick

”Richard…?”
”…!”
”Come.”